WITHDRAWN

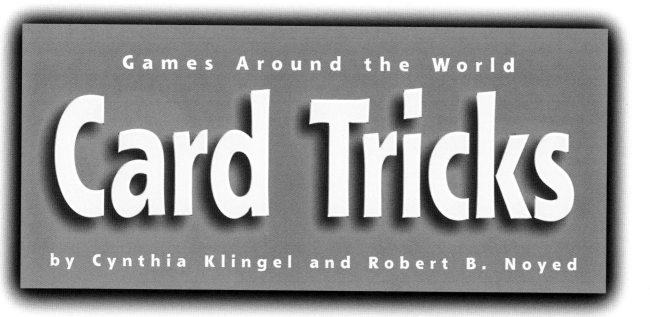

Games Around the World

Card Tricks

by Cynthia Klingel and Robert B. Noyed

Content Adviser: Philip Willmarth, International Brotherhood of Magicians

Social Science Adviser: Professor Sherry L. Field, Department of Curriculum and Instruction, College of Education, The University of Texas at Austin

Reading Adviser: Dr. Linda D. Labbo, Department of Reading Education, College of Education, The University of Georgia

COMPASS POINT BOOKS

MINNEAPOLIS, MINNESOTA

Compass Point Books
3722 West 50th Street, #115
Minneapolis, MN 55410

Visit Compass Point Books on the Internet at *www.compasspointbooks.com* or e-mail your request to *custserv@compasspointbooks.com*

Photographs ©: Gregg Andersen, cover, 5, 10, 11, 26, 27; Catherine Karnow/Corbis, 4; Stock Montage, 6; Victoria & Albert Museum, London/Art Resource, N.Y., 7; Bettmann/Corbis, 9; Hirz/Hulton Getty/Archive Photos, 12.

Editors: E. Russell Primm and Emily J. Dolbear
Photo Researchers: Svetlana Zhurkina and Jo Miller
Photo Selector: Emily J. Dolbear
Designer: Bradfordesign, Inc.
Illustrator: Brandon Reibeling

Library of Congress Cataloging-in-Publication Data

Klingel, Cynthia Fitterer.
    Card tricks / by Cynthia Klingel and Robert Noyed.
        p. cm. — (Games around the world)
    Includes bibliographical references (p.) and index.
    Summary: Presents a history of cards and card tricks, along with tips and easy step-by-step instructions for performing several tricks.
    ISBN 0-7565-0190-3 (hardcover)
        1. Card tricks—Juvenile literature. [1. Card tricks. 2. Magic tricks.] I. Noyed, Robert B. II. Title. III. Series.
    GV1549 .K53 2002
    793.8'5—dc21   2001004745

Table of Contents

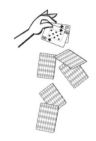

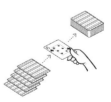

Houses, Games, or Tricks

You can build a towering building with them. You can play games with a group of friends with them. Or you can play games alone with them. You can even do magic tricks with them. Can you guess what they are? They are playing cards, of course!

Many magicians use cards to do tricks. In some tricks, cards seem to move

▲ A boy holds all his cards in one hand.

4

around in the **deck** as if by magic. In other tricks, the magician surprises everyone by guessing which card was chosen by a **volunteer**. Card tricks fool people who don't know the secrets.

Would you like to make some magic with cards? First let's find out more about cards. Then we'll learn how to surprise and amaze people with a simple deck of cards!

▲ *Building a house of playing cards*

5

The History of Cards

People have probably used playing cards for more than 1,000 years. It is believed that people first played cards in Egypt, China, or perhaps India.

No one can be sure how playing cards came to Europe. We know they appeared in Italy by 1299.

In the 1500s, the French people played with a deck of fifty-two cards.

▲ A box of Indian playing cards from the 1800s

◀ Wealthy European cardplayers from the 1400s

The French cards had diamonds, hearts, spades, and clubs on them. The Germans played with a deck of thirty-two cards. The Spanish deck had forty cards.

Early playing cards cost a lot of money. These cards were made and painted by hand. Only kings, queens, and other wealthy people used them.

Playing cards became popular after the printing press was invented. Then cards were easier to make and cost less to buy. Today, people around the world use cards to play many different kinds of games.

Playing cards have been used by magicians for hundreds of years. In the 1800s, a

Money Cards

In North America, playing cards were sometimes used as money. In 1685, Canada used playing-card money. For more than fifty years, the government gave out cards with values marked on them.

French magician named Jean-Eugène Robert-Houdin used cards in many of his magic tricks. He is known as the "Father of Modern Magic." Many of Robert-Houdin's card tricks are still used today.

In the 1900s, an American magician named Harry Houdini did card tricks. He took his name from the great Robert-Houdin! At one time, people called Harry Houdini the "King of Cards."

▲ *Jean-Eugène Robert-Houdin doing a magic trick*

9

Learning about Cards

A modern deck of playing cards has fifty-two cards plus two **jokers**. Playing cards are made of two pieces of thin cardboard glued together. The back of each card has the same pattern. The other side of a card is called the **face.**

A deck of cards has four **suits.** They are hearts, diamonds, clubs, and spades. The hearts and diamonds are red. The clubs and spades are black.

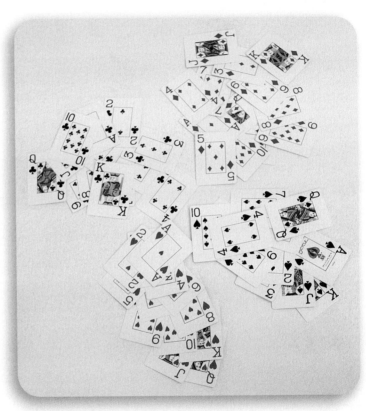

▲ *A standard deck has thirteen cards of each suit.*

Each suit has thirteen cards. There are ten **numbered cards** and three **face cards.** The ace card is the number

▲ *The jack, the king, and the queen are the face cards.*

one card. The other cards are numbered two through ten.

The face cards have pictures on them. The "J" card, called the jack, comes after the "10" card. The "Q" card, called the queen, comes after the jack. The "K" card, called the king, is the highest face card.

Card Trick Tips

For most card tricks, all you need is a deck of playing cards. Some card tricks require preparation, though, such as setting up the deck a certain way or making special cards. Always make sure you are prepared before you begin a card trick.

A good magician needs to be a good storyteller, too. Setting the scene and telling a story makes your trick more interesting.

▲ *A magician from the 1960s does a card trick on his arm.*

It helps convince people that you are using magic. It can also distract people from trying to figure out the trick.

Good magicians practice constantly. Practice your tricks until they come naturally to you. Practice telling the stories you will tell during the trick. You might even practice the trick in front of a mirror.

Card Trick Don'ts!

- Don't do a trick for people until you are sure you can do it properly.

- Don't do the same trick two times in a row. People might figure out your trick!

- Don't explain how you do a trick. Simply say, "It's magic!"

Some card-trick magicians like to dress up. A hat and a flowing cape or large coat are fun to wear. A costume makes your magic trick more dramatic!

Key Card

Magicians often use a **key card** in their card tricks. A key card is a known card in a known place in the deck. That place is often the top or bottom of the deck.

Setup:

1. Choose a key card.

2. Put it facedown on the bottom of the deck.

Trick:

1. Ask a volunteer to choose a card from the deck. Tell the volunteer to remember the chosen card. Remind him or her not to tell you the card!

▲ Ask your volunteer to pick a card.

14

2.	**Cut** the deck into two piles.

3.	Put the chosen card on top of the pile that does not include the key card.

4.	Put the pile that includes the key card on top of the other pile. (Now the key card will be on top of the chosen card.)

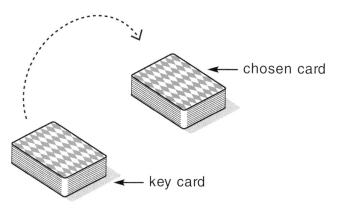

chosen card

key card

▲ *Put the key card pile on top of the chosen card pile.*

5.	Ask the volunteer to cut the cards and complete the cut again. Cutting the cards again helps to "be sure the card is lost in the deck." Actually, cutting the deck almost never separates the key card from the chosen card.

15

6. Ask the volunteer to turn the cards over one by one on the table. Ask the volunteer to help you by concentrating on the chosen card.

7. When the volunteer turns over the key card, prepare to shout "That's it!" the moment you see the next card in the deck.

▲ When you see the key card, the next card will be the chosen card!

Finder Magic

In the Finder Magic trick, the magician uses the key card in a more dramatic way.

Setup:

1. Use a full deck of cards, facedown.

2. Place a six card—faceup—on the bottom of the deck.

3. Put five cards—facedown—under the six at the bottom of the deck.

Trick:

1. Tell your friend that you will magically find any card he or she chooses.

▲ *Setting up the Finder Magic trick*

2. Spread the deck out on the table. Make sure to keep the faceup six hidden.

3. Ask your friend to pick any card—and remember it.

4. Now pile the cards back together. Be careful not to let the faceup six show.

5. Ask your friend to put the chosen card facedown on top of the pile of cards.

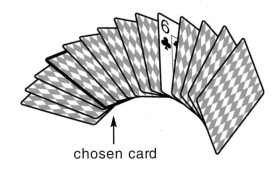

chosen card

▲ *After you cut the deck, the chosen card will be the sixth card after the six card.*

6. Cut the deck. Then pick up the other bottom half and put it on top of the pile of cards. Again, be careful not to show the faceup six.

7. Announce that after you snap your fingers, a card in the middle of the deck will magically turn over. This magic "finder card" will lead you to your friend's card.

8. **Fan** out the deck. The six will appear, faceup.

9. Announce that this magic finder card is telling you where your friend's card is. It is six cards below the finder card.

10. Count down six cards from the finder card. Turn that card over, and shout, "It's magic!"

▲ *Don't forget to shout "It's magic!"*

Returning Pair

The Returning Pair trick will convince your friends that you can move cards magically!

Setup:

1. Remove four cards—the eight and nine of clubs and the eight and nine of spades—from the deck.

2. Put the nine of clubs on the top of the deck.

3. Now put the nine of spades and the eight of clubs on top of the deck.

4. Put the eight of spades on the bottom of the deck.

▲ *Setting up the Returning Pair trick*

Trick:

1. Tell your friend that you can make a pair of cards return to your hand after burying them in the deck.

2. Quickly turn over the top two cards. Show them for only a moment. This is the key to the trick. Also, don't say the names of the cards. Place the two cards in the middle of the deck.

3. Announce that when you tap the deck, the cards will return to your hand. Tap the deck.

▲ *Pinch your fingers and grab the top and bottom cards!*

4. Hold the deck with your thumb and forefinger. Pinch your fingers together, grabbing the top and bottom

21

cards of the deck. These two cards will stay between your fingers. Jerk your hand as you pinch the top and bottom cards. The rest of the deck will fall to the table. This is a tricky move. You will have to practice it alone first.

5. Quickly display the two cards in your fingers. Announce that you have moved the cards magically from the middle of the deck into your fingers. Your friend will of course think they are the same cards you showed at the beginning of the trick!

Airborne Magic

The Airborne Magic trick requires extra time to set up—and two packs of the same cards. In this trick, the magician guesses what a card will do!

What you need: Two cards of the same suit and number, a tube of glue or rubber cement, any thirty cards from a deck, a pencil, a piece of paper, and a paper bag

Setup:

1. Carefully glue the backs of the two cards together. Line them up so that they look like only one card. This is now the "special card."

▲ *Making the "special card"*

2. Place this card in the middle of your pile of cards.

Trick:

1. Show all the faces of the cards. Make sure no one sees the backs of the cards. If they do, they will notice that the special card doesn't have a back!

2. Announce that you are going to throw the pile of cards into the air several times. Each time, you will remove all cards that land facedown. At the end of the trick, one card will be left facing up. Tell everyone that you will now guess what that card will be.

3. Ask for a volunteer.

4. Write the suit and number of your special card on the piece of paper with the pencil. Fold the paper and give it to the volunteer.

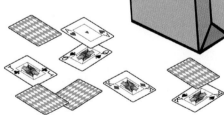

▲ Remove all the cards that land facedown.

5. Now give all the cards, faceup, and the paper bag to the volunteer. Have the volunteer drop the cards into the bag, shake them up, and dump them out.

6. Pick up the cards that land faceup. Put them back in the bag. Push the facedown cards aside.

7. Repeat this process until you have one card left. Don't be discouraged if it takes a long time to end up with just one faceup card. The longer it takes, the more impossible your trick will seem.

▲ *The last card will be your special card!*

8. Then ask the volunteer to read the suit and number of the card aloud. Smile as the volunteer announces that you guessed the right card!

Learning Card Tricks

You can try many different card tricks. Some are easier than others. The hardest tricks often surprise people most.

Now that you know how to do a few card tricks, keep practicing. It takes a lot of practice to do a trick well. With enough practice, you can become a real magician.

You and your friends can have fun with a deck of cards in so many ways. The most fun can be performing magic!

▲ *Don't forget to practice your card tricks!*

Glossary

cut—to divide a deck of cards

deck—a set, or pack, of cards

face—the front of a card

face cards—jacks, queens, and kings in a deck of cards

fan—to spread the cards out like an open fan

jokers—extra playing cards with a court jester on them, used in some games as the wild cards or the highest-ranked cards

key card—a known card in a known place in the deck, used to locate a particular card or cards

numbered cards—the cards from one (ace) through ten

suit—one of the four sets of cards that make up a deck—spades, hearts, diamonds, or clubs

volunteer—an assistant from the audience

Did You Know?

 In the past, magicians threw scaling cards out into the audience. Scaling cards were made of heavier paper and used to advertise things.

 The most expensive single playing card sold for $7,450 in 1990.

 Europe has special clubs for people who collect only jokers from packs of cards.

 The tallest house of cards was 25 feet (7.6 meters) tall. Bryan Berg built this house of cards in Berlin, Germany, in 1999. He used more than 2,000 decks of cards and no glue!

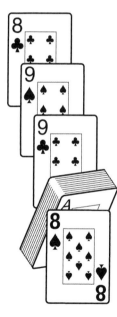

Want to Know More?

At the Library

Fulves, Karl. *Easy-to-Do Card Tricks for Children.* New York: Dover Publications, 1991.

Longe, Bob. *Easy Card Tricks.* London: Sterling Publications, 1995.

Longe, Bob, and Jennifer A. Kelley. *Card Tricks Galore.* London: Sterling Publications, 1999.

Railing, John, and Doris Ettlinger. *Ten Awesome Card Tricks.* New York: Troll Communications, 1998.

On the Web

Card Trick Central

http://web.superb.net/cardtric/

For more easy card tricks and useful links

Magicians' Biographies

http://www.magictricks.com/bios/whoswho.htm

For information about the lives of famous magicians

Tribute to Houdini

http://www.houdinitribute.com

For photographs, information, and a quiz about Harry Houdini's life

Through the Mail

The Houdini Historical Center

330 East College Avenue

Appleton, WI 54911

To request information about famous magician Harry Houdini

On the Road

Beinecke Rare Book and Manuscript Library

At the corner of Grove and High Streets

New Haven, CT 06520-8240

http://www.library.yale.edu/beinecke/brblinfo.htm

To see Yale University's collection of playing cards from many different countries

Index

About the Author

Cynthia Klingel has worked as a high school English teacher and an elementary school teacher. She is currently the curriculum director for a Minnesota school district. Cynthia Klingel lives with her family in Mankato, Minnesota.

Robert B. Noyed started his career as a newspaper reporter. Since then, he has worked in school communications and public relations at the state and national level. Robert B. Noyed lives with his family in Brooklyn Center, Minnesota.